HOW TO
PRAY
WHEN
HEALING
DOESN'T HAPPEN

This book is not intended to provide medical advice or to take the place of medical advice and treatment from your personal physician. Readers are advised to consult their own doctors or other qualified health professionals regarding the treatment of their medical problems. Neither the publisher nor the author takes any responsibility for any possible consequences from any treatment, action, or application of medicine, supplement, herb, or preparation to any person reading or following the information in this book. If readers are taking prescription medications, they should consult with their physicians and not take themselves off medicines to start supplementation without the proper supervision of a physician.

For permission requests, write to the publisher at the address below.

Yorkshire Publishing
4613 E. 91st St,
Tulsa, OK 74137
www.YorkshirePublishing.com
918.394.2665

Printed in the USA

HOW TO
PRAY
WHEN
HEALING
DOESN'T HAPPEN

A Guide and Advanced Training for Mind/Body Healing

Craig A. Miller

T U L S A

Contents

Introduction

The advanced healing steps training program was written because many people asked for more information about how to use these prayer interventions for healing mind/body conditions. The primary focus is teaching how to pray when healing does not happen after using initial prayers for healing, unforgiveness, sins, and spiritual warfare issues. (For more on the subject of initial healing prayers, read *Finding Victory When Healing Doesn't Happen*, by Dr. Randy Clark and Craig Miller).

The unique part of using these healing steps is that you do not need to change the style or method of how your healing ministry or prayer team currently provides healing prayers. The prayers in this book are intended to simply be added to any healing prayer ministry or method. Through God's leading, these have been shown to be very effective in breaking through closed hearts, negative beliefs, emotionally shutdown minds, chronic pain and suffering, or spiritual warfare issues. As a result, God will bring permanent healing to mind and body conditions. For people who have not received healing, receiving permanent healing may seem to be foreign or an unobtainable achievement. However, healing may seem unobtainable because of early unresolved traumatic mind/body experiences that create the belief you cannot be healed.

People who have not received healing often feel discouraged and begin to doubt and question their own faith to be healed. However, God wants healing to be complete by allowing Him to identify and heal any traumatic mind/body experiences that are blocking the healing. One of the purposes of this guidebook is to align with God to make the impossible become possible (see Luke 1:37).

Before you continue with this guidebook, I recommend you read my book, *Breaking Emotional Barriers to Healing*, and/or attend my conference, *How to Pray When Healing Doesn't Happen*. This information will enable you to more effectively follow and understand this training material. As you read the teaching material, throughout this book you will see references in parentheses "(see BEBH, page number)." This indicates the page number where you will find additional information about the specific topic you are reading. The letters "BEBH" indicate my book, *Breaking Emotional Barriers to Healing*. For more information about the *book or conference locations, go to Craig's web site, www.insightsfromtheheart.com.*

As you read, remember that God can heal *anyone, anywhere,* and *anytime.* And, although we may not understand why it seems God does not always answer at the time we pray, our obligation is to continue praying and believing that God loves us enough to want us healed (see Matthew 20:21). This training is dedicated to teaching advanced healing intercession to create more spirit and soul breakthroughs for more effective and permanent healing. All for the glory of God.

PRAYERS FOR RELEASING SOUL TRAUMAS WHEN HEALING DOES NOT HAPPEN

Use these healing steps to:

1. Copy to your cell phone or make a photo copy for a pocket size card to use for prayer with others
2. Use as a reference while you read through this guide book

HEALING STEPS

1. Ask: When did you first have this condition or feeling?
   1a. If reason for condition/feeling is KNOWN-
       Ask: Describe what happened, how it made you feel
   1b. If reason for condition/feeling is NOT KNOWN-
       Ask: Describe feelings while living with the condition and pray to recall early memories with same feelings
2. Ask: The amount you feel the condition in the mind/body (0-10)?
3. Picture safe person in memory protecting/hugging you
4. Command to go: emotional, physical, cellular memory, sight, memory, and hearing trauma, in Jesus' name
5. Declare healing to heart/mind/body in Jesus' name
6. Ask: The amount you now feel the condition in mind/body (0-10)?
7. Praise God for what He has done. Repeat 1-7 as needed
8. Instruct how to believe for healing by focusing on God's Word, not on the condition. Give all hurt to Jesus

Craig Miller©2018—www.insightsfromtheheart.com

Change How You Think About Healing

- If healing does not happen, shift your thinking from the symptoms you see or feel to identifying the root or cause of the condition. What you see and feel is only the result of something deeper. The healer should always expand the search to find the root issues that created the symptoms. For example, as odd as it may sound, the reason for unsuccessful healing of long-term neck pain is rarely an issue about the neck but, rather, it lies with unresolved issues of someone or something that has been an aggravation in life and "a pain in the neck!" (See BEBH, 141.)

- Since illness, pain, and unhealthy emotion are not from God and the Bible states you are as a wonderful creation, made in God's image, that means anything not of God is not intended to be a part of you and is not part of your identity. If it is not God's design or plan, that means someone or some event gave you this condition and you do not need to keep it or let it be a part of you. From now on, think of illness, pain, and unhealthy emotion as a foreign object that you can give away. Whatever was given to you that is unhealthy, you now have the choice to release it because it is not yours to keep.

- Everything has a cause, root, or origin. If you provided traditional prayer for releasing sin, unforgiveness, and generational spiritual issues, and the condition or unhealthy emotion is still present, the next step would be to expand your search to find the root origin of the soul trauma. (This will be explained under Healing Step 2.)

- The longer a person has been experiencing the unhealthy emotional or physical symptoms, the more likely it is that the person has adjusted their thinking and behaviors to live with these symptoms. As a result, the person may have difficulty releasing the symptoms for one or both of the following reasons:

   1. The person may worry that the symptoms will return and feels more in control of the situation with the symptoms than without.
   2. The person has learned to live with the symptoms and does not know how to live without them.

   The healer can begin the healing steps by listening to how the person describes their worries if the symptoms return or fears to live without the symptoms.

- Adult negative reactions are unresolved early-life hurtful experiences that have been held inside (suppressed). These early hurtful experiences will come out during adult situations that trigger those suppressed emotions. Releasing the early hurt will eliminate the adult negative responses.

- The word *wound* is the English translation of the Greek word *trauma*, which is why I use the word "trauma" throughout the book and when I pray for healing. You can still use words such as hurt, wounded, injured, abused, mistreated, or others, but they are all describing trauma (see BEBH, 20-21).

• During the healing steps the person will tell you about many hurtful experiences. The following definitions will help you learn about each trauma (see BEBH, 21-22).

Cellular memory trauma: With every physical trauma there is cellular memory trauma to the body. When there is physical trauma to the body, your tissues, cells, muscles, ligaments, and organs can hold the memory of the trauma.

Emotional trauma: With every trauma there is always a negative emotion as a result of that traumatic experience. For example, when you are injured in an auto accident there is a physical trauma (i.e., broken leg) and an emotional trauma (ie, fears) from the experience. Emotional trauma also includes insults, name calling, mind games, verbal abuse, and seeing or hearing others being hurt.

Hearing trauma: This is sounds or words that are negative, hurtful, harmful, and abusive.

Memory trauma: This includes any trauma experience that becomes stored in your memory.

Physical trauma: This is any harm/injury to your body from physical or sexual abuse, accidents, injuries, surgeries.

Sight trauma: This is sights that are negative, hurtful, harmful, and abusive.

Indicators That Emotions Are a Barrier to Healing (See BEBH, 55-56)

When healing has not occurred, the following conditions of the mind and body are indicators that emotions may be barriers to healing:

- Injuries causing pain and discomfort that come and go for little or no known reason.
- Aches and pains that appear for no known reason and any pain or discomfort that comes and goes for little or no known reason.
- Long-term chronic conditions that do not improve with prayer or a variety of treatment modalities such as medication, medical treatment, and alternative or supplemental treatments. (It is suggested that some causes of chronic conditions can include reactions to medication, food allergies, food additives, environmental issues such as electric fields, magnetic fields and radio frequencies, cellphones, Wi-Fi, mold, etc.)
- If the person cannot release feelings of being wronged or injured by someone or some entity, including church, workplace, or school (this is

most evident when you hear words such as unfair, unjust, wronged, anger, hurt, want to get even, can't forgive).

- When emotional reactions or the description of the condition is verbalized as if the incident happened a week ago when it actually occurred a year or more ago.
- When there is a personal history of physical, mental, emotional, sexual, spiritual, or financial abuse, or the witnessing of traumatic events such as a house fire, accident, military service trauma, or the loss of an emotionally close relative or pet.
- When experiencing long-term stressful and/or traumatic situations related to medical, physical, financial, occupational, or emotional situations.

Teaching Points: What to do if these indicators are identified

- If any of the aforementioned indicators are present, pray for the Holy Spirit to reveal to the person what emotional and physical problems need to be healed first. Next, use the healing steps with what is revealed.
- If the healer identifies emotional barriers but the person does not feel or believe the emotional indicators are a problem, it is recommended to do the following:

    1. The longer a person lives with the hurt from trauma, the more they will incorporate the feelings into their daily life and minimize the trauma issues. The healing minister should not comment on the person's lack of understanding of their trauma ori-

gin. Continue identifying and releasing the roots of the trauma using the healing steps.

2. If the person has had previous healing ministry, especially if they say, "I have already worked through this issue," this person may not be open to digging deeper into root issues. Tell the person to pretend they have not had ministry or counseling in the past and allow themselves to go anywhere in the past. This statement will give the Holy Spirit and the healing minister more freedom to identify root issues.

Emotions vs spiritual warfare (See BEBH, 51-53)

When Jesus is in your heart, His spirit dwells in you (see 1 Cor. 3:16) and you are already set free (see Galatians 5:1) from evil and darkness (see Colossians 1:13) because Jesus is separated from death and sin (see John 14:6). This means that, if the spirit of Jesus is in you, the evil spirits cannot be in you unless you allow evil to come in through "doors" such as sin and hurtful events. I am not saying you will be automatically affected by evil spirits any time you experience hurt. However, the longer you hold on to unhealthy emotions, the greater the opportunity for evil spirits to enter the open "door" of hurt and make the hurt feel worse.

The good news is that, as a believer, you already have all the power and authority of Jesus to close that door and keep evil out. So, when you release the emotional root, the evil spirit will fall away because it has nothing on which to attach. As a result, when you reveal and release the original trauma, forgive the offender, and replace the hurt with Jesus's love, that closes the door of hurt and restores your soul back to its original state of healthiness.

Since most churches do not traditionally address emotions while praying for healing, many prayer ministers do not ask deep enough questions to uncover the original hurtful events that block healing. As a result, if healing does not happen and the condition persists, prayer ministers often think demonic spirits are the cause, rather than taking the time to identify the original emotion from traumatic issues that blocked healing and allowed evil spirits to harass. Consequently, when emotional trauma is the original problem and the primary barrier to healing, if you begin the healing process with demonic warfare prayers, you may feel some relief and freedom but may not experience full release of the unhealthy emotional issues. As a result, if you only release evil spirits and not the original traumatic emotion, demonic spirits can return, reattach themselves to the emotion, and make the condition worse.

A woman was told evil spirits were harassing her when healing prayer did not get rid of her discouragement and fears. When she said these feelings continued most of her life, God took her to childhood memories with a father who was depressed and often yelled. When the woman pictured Jesus protecting her from her father, she was able to release the childhood hurt. As a result, the feelings of discouragement and fear were released and she felt a happiness she had not felt before. The woman realized the original problem was the childhood negative emotions and evil spirits made her feel worse. When the negative emotion was released, the evil spirits left because they had nothing to attach to.

I have routinely found that entering into healing prayer by revealing the sin and/or emotion from the original trauma has been successful in attaining permanent release and restoring the body and soul with little to no demonic interference. However, if an evil spirit does show itself, you have the authority in Jesus to tell it to leave. Once you help the person release the sin and emotion, the demonic forces do not have a foothold or reason to remain attached, and the door is closed so they cannot return. Starting the healing process by finding the original root of traumatic hurt has shown to be more effective for resolution of the mind/body conditions, and increases the potential of a permanent healing outcome. I recommend your focus and words should primarily be about Jesus and, as a result, this will not give evil the opportunity to gain any rights or allow interference to the healing process.

What to Do When Healing Doesn't Happen

When healing has not happened after using traditional healing prayer which may include forgiveness of sin and forgiving others and yourself, it is time to use the following healing steps for releasing past trauma. These steps will help to expand the search to reveal earlier emotions or memories that may be barriers to the healing process (see BEBH, 122). As a result, when emotional issues from the past are identified and released, the soul will be free to flow in healing. Always ask the Holy Spirit to provide revelation and guidance as you go through the following healing steps.

HEALING STEPS FOR RELEASING
SOUL TRAUMA (See BEBH, 83)

Healing Step 1.

To learn more about the condition, **ask the person, "When did you first remember experiencing this condition or feeling?"** The healer can ask more questions such as, "Was the condition or emotion caused by an event, an offender, or was there no identifiable reason?" The person will typically respond to Healing Step 1 with one of the following answers (see BEBH, 35-38):
a. The trauma that caused the condition is **known** to the person.
b. The trauma that caused the condition is **unknown** to the person.

1a. *Known Trauma*

The trauma is considered known when the person can remember the event or person that caused the condition and identify the past details of the condition.
If the reason for the condition is known:

- **Ask the person: "Describe what happened and how it made you feel."**
- Have the person briefly describe the experience, including the feelings, they had when it happened.
- After the person shares their feelings, **then go to Healing Step 2.**

1b. *Unknown Trauma*

The trauma is considered unknown when the person cannot remember or identify why or who caused the condition and have no known reason for the condition. If the reason for the condition is unknown:

- **Ask the person: "Describe your feelings of living with the condition."**
- Ask them when they first experienced the symptoms, and what stressful events happened to them, or to others , before the symptoms started.
- **Next, ask the person: "Recall early memories that produced similar feelings."**
- After the person recalls their early memories, **then go to Healing Step 2.**

21

HEALING STEPS CONTINUE FROM STEPS 1A OR 1B

Healing Step 2.

After you received information from 1a or 1b, do the following:
Ask the person: "Thinking of the past memory, rate the
amount of hurt you feel now or what you think you felt
in the past memory with the mind/body condition, on
a scale from 0–10 (with 10 being the highest)"

ADVANCE TEACHING FOR HEALING STEPS 1, 1A, 1B, 2

Teaching Point: Using Healing Steps 1, 1a, 1b, 2

When the person describes what it felt like to live with
known or unknown trauma, use the same feeling words
you hear when you ask the person to recall times or events
in the past where he/she felt the same way.

UNKNOWN TRAUMA HEALING TESTIMONY

During Healing Step 1 a woman said she had left arm and
shoulder pain for a year with no explanation. When I asked
what had happened over a year ago, she replied that the family business had had a major loss. This made her feel disap-
pointed, hurt, helpless, deeply sad, very worried about the
future of the family. When we initially prayed for healing and
there was little change, I used Healing Step 2 to expand my
search for past issues by asking her when she felt these feel-

ings earlier in her life. She recalled many incidents where her grandson was very sick and she felt the same feelings. When I prayed for healing using her own words to describe the hurtful emotions, there was only slight improvement.

I again expanded the search by asking where she felt these same feelings as a child. She envisioned her parents having an argument and her mother leaving the home. This woman had these same helpless feelings as she earlier described. I told the woman to envision Jesus standing between her and her parents and she was finally able to release the feelings of helplessness, hurt, and sadness. When I asked her to say, "I need to let you go, mom and dad, and give you to Jesus," she started sobbing. She said she felt it was her job to protect her family. After she was able to release her childhood feelings of helplessness, hurt, and sadness to Jesus, the burden of responsibility was lifted. At the same moment, she noticed the arm and shoulder pain was gone.

What to do when a person cannot identify feelings or think of any hurtful events during Healing Steps 1a, 1b, and 2 (See BEBH,103,105)

When someone experiences excessive unhealthy emotions at the time of the trauma, the mind may not be able to properly process all the information. As a result, emotions, images, sounds, and physical sensations become stuck in a traumatic state in the mind. When this happens, the mind suppresses (holds in) the information to protect itself from overload or shock. This is usually the reason a person will not be able to identify feelings or remember past hurtful events. The suppressed emotions become a barrier to healing unless you help the person identify and release the suppressed feelings. Although God can break through that shock and heal the trauma, God also created a free will to choose what to do with your emotions. He will not condemn or manipulate your decision to hold on to the emotions or memories if your mind or body is not ready to release them. The mind will continue to hold on to the hurtful emotion the rest of your life unless you feel safe enough to release it. The following will explain how to release suppressed thoughts and feelings during healing ministry:

- The mind *can* process properly when the amount and intensity of sensory information can be managed and integrated into the mind for current or future reactions. As a result, the person that has had more opportunities to safely release emotions throughout their life, will be more able to remember memories and identifying emotions during the healing steps. The goal of the healer is to help the person process through the emotion that is identified in their past traumatic memory. This is accomplished by having the person find their feelings from their experiences (see Healing Step 1a, 1b, 2) and give the feelings to their safe person (see Healing Step 3).

- The mind *cannot* process properly when the amount and intensity of sensory information are more than the mind can process and manage at one time, especially if you have no one there to help you process the information. This is when the mind can automatically shut down to protect against further damage or shock and the point when the person becomes emotionally stuck at the age the mind shut down. This means that the emotion, thinking, and behaviors become frozen at the age when the traumatic experience occurred. As a result, when the person feels a hurt in adulthood that is similar to the earlier hurt, they will automatically feel and respond or behave similarly as they would have at that earlier age. Responding with child-like feelings and behaviors will continue the rest of their life, unless that trauma is released. The person typically does not see this behavior in themselves because they are consumed with blaming everyone else for making them feel that way. The role of the healer is to identify the childhood words and behaviors that you hear or see when the person describes their condition (see Healing Steps 1a and 2).

Teaching Points: How to identify unknown feelings and memories for Healing Steps 1a, 1b, and 2

- During the healing steps, if the person cannot remember the past events or emotions, the following simple steps will help the person recall or begin to connect with the past:
  1. Have the person close their eyes and picture themselves, as a child or teen, as if they are watching a movie of themselves in the home and/or school in which they were raised.
  2. As they watch the movie, ask them to guess what they would see and feel living in the unhealthy home situation with other family members. Keep asking more questions about what they guess the situation and feelings would have been like. For example, ask if there was any yelling, arguing, teasing, negative comments, time spent alone, hurt from siblings or schoolmates, etc. Next, ask the person to guess how those experiences would make him/her feel. Proceed with the healing steps using the negative experiences and feelings you uncovered during this time.

- Another reason a person may have difficulty identifying and releasing past thoughts and feelings is because they continue to feel unsafe. Even if the person is sitting in a safe place at the moment of the healing ministry, emotions from past trauma can be strong enough to make the person feel they are still unsafe. If the person felt afraid and unsafe at the time of the original trauma, they will carry the same unsafe feeling into adulthood until that original feeling is released. For example, since a child is learning how to process sensory information at a primitive level, any conflict with a parent has the potential to increase the emotional response of fear. Each fear response will be held in the body and mind until the child believes the environment is safe again to release those feelings. If the person never feels safe, the fear response has the potential to show up later in life as emotional issues, such as anxiety or phsyical issues, such as stomach ailments. The goal of the healer is to help the person feel safe enough to release the emotion that is identified from their past.

For example, if the parents' arguing turns into yelling, screaming threats, or someone storming out of the house, then the combination of emotional, hearing, sight, and mental trauma will make the environment seem unsafe. As a result, the child's mind cannot process the overwhelming sensory information and the emotional and mental systems will shut down. The fears created during the overwhelming early experiences will be felt the rest of their life during similar adult situations (unless the person can feel safe to release the emotion).

Teaching Points: How to help the person feel safe during Healing Steps 1b, 2 and 3

- During the Healing Steps 2 and 3, if the person has difficulty releasing feelings, does not stop talking about the same childhood feelings, or continues to feel unsafe, you can choose to do one of the following:
  1. The healer can use these options to increase a feeling of being safe in the image:
     a) If the person has a strong faith, ask if Jesus would make them feel safe or if they want to request God to assign angels to bring protection and healing. (Tell the person, "If you have never actually felt comforted by Jesus, you are welcome to think of a person to comfort you.)
     b) Ask the person to think of another person that is or has been in their life that has comforted or made them safe.
     c) The person can either replace the previous safe person with a new one or continue to add new many safe people to the image.
     d) If there is no safe person, tell the person, "Picture yourself in a "bullet-proof" bubble with thick glass that separates you from the unsafe people or event. You can see the people but they cannot touch you." If the person agrees, have them see Jesus (or another safe person in the bubble with them.)
  2. After the person initiates one of the above options, have the person think of the hurt and use the Love Hug and Love Pat (Healing Step 3) until there is some change in the image or feeling.

- If the emotional issues cannot be resolved or the emotional or ministry experience is more than can be handled during ministry, it is recommended the person seek professional mental health services.

How to quickly determine what issues from the past are blocking the healing

The best way for the healer to expand the search to find any early events and emotions that are blocking healing is to listen to the words that describe the problem and the location of the condition. The healer will be able to more quickly determine the person's past unhealthy issues by using the following:

1. One way to determine the past unhealthy issues is to listen to the person's words that are used to describe their condition and feelings.
    *   The words will give away the origin of the original traumatic events because the person will usually react using words similar to the age at which they experienced the original trauma (see BEBH,123). As I previously mentioned, if the person was not able to feel safe enough to release the negative experiences in childhood, the feelings would be suppressed and come out in adulthood.

For example, the following adult negative words indicate unresolved hurtful childhood experiences: doubt, can't, unfair, afraid, hopeless, helpless, stuck, not good enough, I'm bad, unwanted, nobody loves me, unworthy, empty, unloved, inadequate, stupid, dumb (see BEBH, 30). As a result, these negative words or phrases are also an indication the person has suppressed memories and emotions from past events.

Teaching Points: How to determine what issues are blocking the healing

- Since negative words represent feelings that originated during the early hurtful experiences, the healer needs to identify the past hurtful experience that is similar to the words and feelings used as an adult. Go through the healing steps, starting with Healing Step 1.
- Use the same words you heard the person say when you take the person back to the past where they first felt these same feelings. For example, if the person currently feels helpless in an adult situation, you may say, "In the past, when did you have a similar feeling of being helpless or afraid?"

---

2. Another way to determine the past issues is to watch where the person describes the location of the condition in the body (see BEBH,125).
   - Since God created each body part and emotion with a vibrational energy frequency, if the unhealthy emotion is not released, the unhealthy emotion will attach itself to the body part that has the same frequency. The unhealthy emotion will then cause disease and

prevent or block the body part from healing (see BEBH, 38).

- When the person identifies the location of the condition, the healing can start with the appropriate healing step to identify and release the original reason for the condition. For example:

If the person identifies a physical condition—listen and watch where the person says the condition is <u>located in their body</u>. The person may say, *My back has been hurting for many months and I don't know why.* Since the condition is identified in the *back*, the healer can identify the connection to body part function and emotion and do the following to begin the healing steps:

A. Find the body part and the emotional connections to that body part on the chart example on page 35 or see BEBH, 141 for a detailed list.

B. Using the chart, the healer can ask the person if any of the emotional connections for that body part are true for them. [Since most of the time lack of emotional support is the origin for long term back problems, it is best to use the healing steps with that emotional issue.]

C. The healer can begin with Healing Step #1b to ask the person to search in their past for the times they had experienced lack of emotional support.

- If the person identifies an emotional condition— listen to what emotion the person says and ask where the person feels the emotion is <u>located in</u>

their body. The person may say, *I have been anxious for years and I feel it mostly in my stomach.* Since the condition is identified in the *stomach*, the healer can identify the connection to body part function and emotion and do the following to begin the healing steps:

A. Find the body part and the emotional connections to that body part on the chart example on page 35 or see BEBH, 141 for a detailed list.

B. Using the chart, the healer can ask the person if any of the emotional connections for that body part are true for them. For example, since the majority of adult anxiety symptoms are created from earlier scary experiences, it is best to find other anxiety experiences from the past.

C. The healer can begin with Healing Step 1b to ask the person to search in their past for the times they had scary experiences.

3. The healer can combine what they observe and hear to connect the emotion with the mind/body condition negative emotions that are stored in the body parts (organs, cells, muscles, tendons, etc.) will increase susceptibility to illness, block healing, or make a current condition worse in that body location. Healing will take place when the person uses the healing steps to identify and release the negative emotions from the body part (BEBH, 27).

    •   During Healing Steps 1 and 2, when the person identifies the body part and/or emotion, the healer can determine the emotional connection to mind/body condition by using the information as shown in the chart example on page 35.

- The following diagram shows how to connect the emotion and body during the healing steps.

During Healing Step 1

The person describes:	The healer determines:	The healer begins Healing Step 1b:
Pain in their **back** ⟶	The condition originated from **lack of emotional support** (See chart on page 35) ⟶	The person searches for **lack of emotional support** in their past

During Healing Step 1

The person describes:	The healer determines:	The healer begins Healing Step 1b:
Feelings of **anxiety** ⟶	The feelings originated from **childhood experiences** (See chart on page 35) ⟶	The person searches for **anxiety** in their past experiences

The following chart shows the most common body part or conditions and their connection to the functon and mind/body issues (For a more detailed list of conditions and emotions see BEBH, 141):

EMOTIONAL CONNECTION TO MIND/BODY CONDITIONS

AFFECTED BODY PART/CONDITION	FUNCTION—EMOTIONAL CONNECTION THAT BLOCKS HEALING
Back/spine	Structural support—Lack of emotional support
Bladder	Releasing, control—Peeved, little control of life
Feet	Movement forward—Fear, difficulty going forward in life
Heart	Feeling life and joy—Hard to find or lost joy, deep hurt
Kidney	Cleaning body, having control— Fear, dread, resentment
Knee	Movement forward, steady—Fear, unmet needs (stuck in life)
Liver	Cleansing body—Anger, frustration
Lung	Breathing is life giving—Grief, loss
Shoulder/neck	Carrying responsibilities and burdens, aggravated
Stomach	Disgusted, nervous, despair
Anxiety	Being alert, cautious—Past helplessness/fear/trauma, no control

Teaching Points: Connecting the emotion to mind/body conditions during the healing steps

Whether the person has a known or unknown trauma, one of the primary reason for not being healed is due to suppressed soul issues, such as suppressed emotions. Healing will take place when you identify and release the emotion associated with the condition. Consider the following when using Healing Steps 1 and 2:

- If the person tells you the condition (such as back pain) but cannot identify the feelings, find the condition and corresponding emotions located in my book (see BEBH, 141). Then go through Healing Steps 1a, 1b, and 2.
- If the person can identify the emotions (such as anxiety, pain, etc.) or the condition (such as a backache), but does not know the cause, ask the person what it is like to live with this condition and then ask the person to recall early memories that produced similar feelings (this is Healing Step 1b).
- Always use the same feeling words you hear when you ask the person to recall times or events in the past where they felt the same way.

HEALING TESTIMONY FOR CONNECTING THE EMOTIONS AND BODY PART

For eight months a woman could not breathe, struggled to swallow, felt tightness in her throat, and was getting worse to the point she said air could not move in her lungs. She was admitted to the hospital for five days, diagnosed with bronchitis, put on eight different antibiotics, and went on sick leave from work. When I asked what had happened eight months ago, she remembered being devastated by the death of her grandfather. When I prayed for God to heal her emotional loss and lungs, there was little change. I expanded my search by asking what else she felt during the time of her loss. I learned the woman felt very helpless and guilty that she could not help or do more for her grandfather. She witnessed her grandfather being put on a ventilator and felt more helpless. "There was nothing I could do. It was so unfair," she said.

Since I knew the words "helpless" and "unfair" were from unresolved childhood issues, I asked when she felt this way in the past. Growing up, she suppressed all her feelings, and was not allowed to talk. She felt very sad and helpless to prevent her parents from fighting. "I couldn't do anything about the fighting, it was so unfair," she replied. The woman did not see the correlation between her similar feelings in childhood and now as an adult. Her unresolved feelings in childhood compounded the grief, helpless feeling, and hurt of losing her grandfather. When she let go of her childhood feelings and forgave her parents, she was immediately able to release and forgive her grandfather for dying. After a very simple prayer, her lungs suddenly opened and she was able to breathe with no restrictions.

HEALING STEPS CONTINUED
FROM STEP 2

↓

Healing Step 3.

Instruct the person to: "Picture a safe person or Jesus in your memory standing between you and the offending person/situation protecting/hugging you or hugging yourself within a protective bubble if you do not have a safe person" (using the Love Hug, see BEBH, 88-89).

Teaching Point: Using Healing Step 3

Suppressed hurts and trauma lock in the physical or emotional condition in the body. A primary reason people cannot suppress hurts is that they did not feel safe, comforted, or loved at the time of the original experience. The purpose of the Love Hug and Love Pat is to create an experience of safety, comfort, and love in order to release the suppressed emotion and subsequently unlock the physical and emotional condition to free the body to function normally with the healing process. *"Come to Me, all who are weary and burdened, and I will give you rest. ...and you will find rest for your soul"* (Matt 11:28-29).

Using the Love Hug and Love Pat

One of the best ways for the person to feel safe is to actually experience the feeling of love and comfort through a simple method called the "Love Hug" (see BEBH, 88-89). The proven prayers of the Love Hug and Love Pat will break emotional barriers by doing the following:

1. They stimulate sensory nerve endings to naturally produce feel-good chemicals and pain suppressors that calm the brain and body. As a result, the person will respond more quickly to release deep trauma and restore vital pathways for receiving soul/body/spirit restoration. This gentle touching stimulates the body, which results in the brain producing dopamine (stimulant), endorphins (pain suppressor), morphine (pleasure chemical and natural opioid), and serotonin (natural antidepressant). God created these brain reactions to happen in a millisecond to help the person feel enough safety and comfort to release the suppressed emotions "... *lay hands on sick, and they will recover*" (Mark 16:18).

2. They create and increase experiences of comfort, safety, and love automatically breaking down walls or barriers that block healing. For example, think

of a small child two to four years old who is playing and having fun. Then suddenly the child falls, scrapes a knee, and starts crying from the pain. You see their eyes filled with tears as they hold the knee. Your heart becomes filled with compassion as you put your arms around them to bring comfort and let them know they are safe. As they begin telling their story between each tear, your gentle pats on the back bring a calming peace to their distress. The more they share the story, the calmer they become. The longer you give them a reassuring hug, the faster the problem suddenly seems *all better now*. As quickly as the pain was experienced, the child returns to a feeling of joy and goes back to playing. As the hug provided comfort, the child felt safe enough to release their thoughts and feelings.

3. God designed the brain to naturally process and release the sensory information that subsequently allows the body to freely release anything that hinders the natural process of healing. A parent's primary function is to teach children how to trust, love, care, express, and behave. *"Train up a child in the way he should go, even when he grows older, he will not abandon it"* (Proverb 22:6).

Your wellness is related to how you learn to deal with stress early in your life. According to Dr. Kenneth Pelletier, MD, *Mind as Healer, Mind as Slayer,* "...stressful experiences, especially in childhood, create within you certain methods of coping with your problems which become the routine for how you will handle stress later in life. 'When this high stress level is prolonged and [not changed], it produces alterations in neurophysiological functioning which can create the preconditions for the development of a disorder.'" As healers, our role is to use the Healing Steps to identify and release the early stressful experiences and related emotion to bring permanent healing.

What to Do When A Person Cannot Release Feelings

- People will struggle to release the suppressed hurt from a past experience unless there is an equal or greater safe experience (during healing ministry) to feel safe enough to release the hurt.

- The younger the age and the more intense the trauma that is experienced, the greater amount of comfort and safety that is needed to release the feelings from the original trauma.

- The longer you have been holding on to hurtful emotions, the more the emotions are incorporated into your belief, thinking, and way of life. As a result, the person may struggle to release what has been so much a part of their life and will have a greater need for safety, comfort, and love to release the feelings.

Teaching Points: When a person cannot release feelings

When the person says they feel numb, stuck, or unable to let go, the following are several different ways to break through to help them release feelings:

- Increase their feeling of comfort and safety by thinking of a significant person (other than Jesus or parents) who has provided comfort to the hurting person at some time in their life. Also, it would be important to place Jesus in the image to give away the hurt and provide the power to bring healing. If they have no safe person in their life, think of being inside a bullet-proof bubble with Jesus.

- Another option is to have the person imagine themselves as an adult coming into the early image by pretending to be a loving parent or older sibling figure hugging the child in the memory. Have the adult person use reassuring words to the child, "I'm sorry you had to go through this," or "Give me your hurt," etc.

- Another option is to find a hurtful experience earlier than the memory you are currently using. For example, if the person cannot release the emotion for a memory he/she is remembering at 10 years old, there is typically a trauma at an earlier age that has greater intensity, which is blocking the 10-year-old memory. Ask God to take the person back to an earlier hurtful experience with similar feelings.

- Another option is to have the person pretend they are watching a movie of themselves in the past and guess what it is like to live in their home or school. Have the person use the Love Hug/Love Pat as they think of the past. Continue the Love Pat until thoughts come to mind. Ask more questions about the past home situation as thoughts come up.

- If the person cannot release feelings of being wronged or injured by someone or something, including church, workplace, or school (remember that this is most evident when you hear words such as; unfair, unjust, wronged, anger, hurt, want to get even, can't forgive), then expand your search to find similar feelings from being wronged or hurt earlier in life. Use the Healing Steps 1 and 2 to find the earlier memories and feelings.

Optional Visual Release

When we experience overwhelming trauma, the sensory information is stored in the body and mind. God created the mind to hold on to the information until we are ready and able to release it. God also created the right and left sides of our brain to handle and store different types of information. Since God will not release what your mind decides to keep, the suppressed memories will remain stuck inside your mind until you decide to find the memory and release it.

God created the natural ability to release sensory information through simple ways such as dreaming and looking to the right or left (see BEBH, 90-91). For example, if you have ever seen a person looking up to the right or left after you ask a question, that is when the person is naturally looking to those areas of their brain, trying to access the stored information as they answer your question. You can use what God naturally created to assist sensory and memory release by simply looking to the right or left during the healing steps.

Teaching Points: Steps to use the visual release

As you view the hurtful event with the safe person during Healing Step 3, do the following to increase the release of unhealthy images and emotion:

- As you are looking forward with your eyes open, imagine the hurtful event in front of you and say what you felt during the event.
- Keeping your head straight (do not move your head), slowly move your eyes to the left and then right to determine which side you feel and see the event more intensely. You can look to the right or left more than once until you determine which side feels more intense.
- Continue looking toward the intense side as you use the Love Hug and Love Pat.
- Continue using the Visual Release as you continue using all the healing steps until the emotion is released.
- When the emotion is released, the person can close their eyes and visualize the safe person giving them a hug and/or feels more positive and reassured.

HEALING STEPS CONTINUED FROM STEP 3

Healing Step 4.

Pray: "In Jesus's name, I release the emotional, physical, sight, hearing, and cellular memory trauma (Option: Give to safe person)." You can declare, "In the name of Jesus I command physical, emotional, and cellular trauma to muscles, tendons, bones to be released. I declare new muscles, tendons, bones, cells to be formed and generated."

ADVANCE TEACHING FOR HEALING STEP 4

Teaching Points: For Healing Step 4

- The person or the healer can use this Healing Step prayer to release the conditions from the mind and body. The person has the option to release it to the safe person or to use the words: release, commanding, cursing, rebuke, or whatever the Holy Spirit gives you to send away the condition. Remember Jesus believed that sickness was not part of God's Kingdom and consequently not part of you. He commanded the sickness to leave.

- Once the healer identifies a hurtful or negative feeling, it is important to identify the trauma event associated with the feeling. You do not need the person to describe the trauma event. Simply have them remember it happened and either command the general trauma to leave (e.g., "In Jesus' name, I command the emotional trauma to leave") or use specific statements, such as commanding the emotional trauma of fear to leave.

- Either the person or the healer may command the trauma to leave but it can be more powerful for the person to verbalize the command. When you confess or release the emotion, you are letting go of the stronghold or power the trauma has over you (see James 5:16).

HEALING TESTIMONY

During ministry using Healing Step 1, a woman said she had suffered from back pain for the last two months. To identify if the cause was known or unknown to her (Healing Step 1a and 1b), I asked what happened three months ago and she said that her back suddenly hurt when she lifted something. The prayers and medical treatment she received did not help. Since I was aware that the emotional connection to back pain is lack of emotional support from some time in life, I asked her to recall an earlier time in her life where she did not feel emotionally supported (this is Healing Step 1b).

I asked the Holy Spirit to take the woman to an earlier time in her life where she did not receive emotional support from someone important to her. The woman described her mother as not being supportive when she was a child. I asked what that felt like as a child and how much that hurt her on a scale from 0 to 10 (this is Healing Step 2). I could see the sadness on her face as she described the feelings of rejection and abandonment because her mother did not show affection. I asked the woman to imagine a safe person while she used the Love Hug and Love Pat and imagine giving the hurt to the safe person and Jesus (this is Healing Steps 3 and 4).After the release, I asked Jesus to bring healing to her body (this is Healing Step #5). I asked what she felt like emotionally/physically, from 0 to 10 (this is Healing Step #6). The woman said the pain was down to a pain level of 3. We praised God for her healing (this is Healing Step 7) and we repeated Healing Steps 1-7. After we repeated the healing steps, the back pain was gone. Although God heard the woman's frequent prayers, the release of her deeper soul issues freed her body and mind to receive her healing.

What to do when the person has overwhelming emotion during their release (See BEBH, 50-51)

Excessive emotion, such as hysterical crying, sobbing, heavy breathing, and dry heaves are often the release of old trauma and emotional pain, rather than a symptom of demonic spirits. (However, you still have the option to use spiritual warfare prayers.)

Teaching Points: What to do when the person has overwhelming emotion

If the person becomes overwhelmed when they release emotion, continue reassuring the person by imagining the safe person and/or Jesus protecting them. You can use the following steps:

1. Reassure the person with active listening and validation (see BEBH, 49)

---

2. At eye level in front of the person, make sure they look at you as you use statements such as:

   "Look at me. Listen to what I'm saying. I hear you are really afraid right now, but you are in _(say your location)_ talking to me. The person you are afraid of is not here. Look where you are. You are safe right now. Repeat after me, 'I am at _(your location)_. I'm not with that person. I am safe.'"

   Refer back to the image of the safe person and/or Jesus being with them as they continue the healing steps.

3. If you detect spiritual warfare, you have the option of binding and commanding any demonic spirit to leave, such as, breaking off generational curses, or rebuking evil strongholds and declaring peace and the blood of Jesus over the person. (This is discussed further in the book, *Finding Victory When Healing Doesn't Happen*, by Randy Clark and myself. Read the section titled "Spiritual Warfare" for more details.) After you briefly command the spirit to leave, return to releasing the negative emotion. You also need to remember that the Evil One is already defeated and is only there because it is attached to something, such as sin or negative emotion. If the person has Jesus in his/her heart, once you release the negative emotions, the Evil One has nothing to attach itself to and must leave.

- If the emotional issues cannot be resolved or the emotional or ministry experience is more than can be handled during ministry, it is recommended the person seek professional mental health services.

HEALING STEPS CONTINUED FROM STEP 4

Healing Step 5.

Declare healing to heart/mind/body in Jesus's name

Healing Step 6.

Ask the person, To rate the amount of hurt
you feel in mind/body now (0-10)?

Healing Step 7.

The healer and/or the person can praise God for the healing.
If the negative feeling or condition is more than zero, you
can repeat healing steps 1 through 7 as needed.

What to do when trauma comes in layers and healing comes in layers (See BEBH, 115-118)

When you need to pray repeatedly over an illness or condition, that is not necessarily a sign of a lack of faith or a weak prayer life, but is usually a sign that there are more issues to be identified and released. If releasing the issues require many prayer sessions because of temporary improvement or symptoms that return the next day or in a few days, it is evidence that there may be multiple events that need to be released. Whether it is multiple events in the situation or separate events that happened through the years of life, each event can represent a new layer and the various hurts in each event can represent another layer.

HEALING TESTIMONY

I ministered to a woman who suffered back, shoulder, and neck hurt at a pain level that was typically a 7 for the last ten years. When I asked what happened ten years ago (this is Healing Step #1), she said she had a car accident. Next, I asked her to describe the feelings that she experienced in the accident (this is Healing Step 1a). When she told me about feeling scared when it happened, especially while driving the car, I asked, 'When you were afraid during the accident, how much did that make you feel on a scale of 0-10?'" (this is Healing Step 2). I had her imagine her grandfather (safe person) and Jesus in the car at the time of the accident; while using the Love Hug and Love Pat, she released the emotional, physical, and memory trauma (this is Healing Steps 3 and 4). We declared healing (this is Healing Step 5) and she said the pain level in her body was down to 4.

The continued pain represented more layers of trauma. We thanked God for the healing and repeated Healing Steps 1-7 by asking God to bring to her the next part of this accident that was hurtful. The woman said the extraction from the car was painful. With that information, I repeated Healing Steps 1-7. During Healing Step 6, her pain level went down to 3. We again asked God to bring to her the next part of this accident that was hurtful. The woman said the ambulance ride was very painful. With that information, I repeated Healing Steps 1-7. During Healing Step 6, her pain level went down to 2. We again asked God to bring to her the next part of this accident that was hurtful. The woman said living with this pain over the last ten years has been a terrible experience. With that information, I repeated Healing Steps 1-6. During Healing Step 6, her pain level went down to 0. We praised God for the healing and instructed her how to live in her healing (this is Healing Steps 7 and 8).

Teaching Points: Steps to use when healing comes in layers

- If there are multiple layers, tell the person the healing process can be like peeling an onion.
- Follow the healing steps to release each hurtful incident (layer).
- Listen and watch for clues to what the Holy Spirit wants you to do as you pray.

Continue to expand your search to identify and release layers, such as the following:

1. The person may tell you many different traumatic events over a period of time. They may include disappointment, loss, and injustices caused by family, friends, work situations, etc.

- Each event should be revealed and released using the healing steps, unless you are led to pray over all the issues in one bundle.

2. The person may tell you multiple traumatic experiences from the same life event.

- If the person senses are overwhelmed with emotion from the effects of multiple traumas during the same event or separate incidents with the same abusive person, such as repeated abuse (e.g., repeated molestation) by the same person or an auto accident with many traumatic experiences (such as, being trapped in the car, having a painful ride to the hospital, seeing someone die, etc.), you will need healing in layers.

- With multiple experiences during the same event, pray for the initial trauma first and then each subsequent layer. This may also include: what happened before the trauma (a loved one suffering), during the trauma (the loved one died), and living with the lasting effects of the trauma (grieving, missing loved one). If the person cannot remember all the layers, start with the earliest memory the person remembers.

- All of these layers should be revealed and released using the healing steps, unless you are led to pray over all the issues in one bundle.

3. If the person has been living a long time with the condition and they have created a life or identity around the condition, it is best to do the following:

- You will need to pray for the initial onset of the trauma, the discomfort of living with the effects of the trauma, the fear and disappointment of not being healed, and the transforming of their mind from living as a unhealthy person to living as a healthy person.

- If the person resists the release of long-term emotion out of fear that they will not receive their healing or out of fear of how they will live differently after they are healed, expand the search for the origin of the fear. Typically, fear is an emotion that originated from childhood experiences.

- Each layer should be revealed and released using the healing steps.

- If the emotional issues cannot be resolved or the emotional or ministry experience is more than can be handled during ministry, it is recommended the person seek professional mental health services.

HEALING STEPS CONTINUED FROM STEP 7

Healing Step 8.

Teach the person how to believe in healing by focusing on God's Word, not on their condition. Encourage them to give Jesus all of their hurt.

55

Teaching Points: How to keep your healing

Most people lose their healing because they do not know how to keep it. Tell the person the following instructions to help them keep their healing:

- Over the next few weeks, you will need to think and act as a healthy person and not as you did as a sick person. Continue any medication or medical treatment until the doctor is consulted.
- Focus on the healing of the condition and not what it was like being sick. For example, if your leg was healed, walk with normal steps, thinking and believing you are healed, rather than the way you walked when you had an illness.
- You can lose your healing if your mind begins to worry or feel any discomfort. Without knowing it, your mind can become consumed by the discomfort. Once you have experienced small pains or thoughts of the former condition, stay in your healing by commanding (in Jesus' name) your pain or unhealthy thoughts to go and reclaim your belief that you are healed.
- If discomfort, pain, or emotional issues (e.g., anxiety) do not go away, that is an indication there are more layers to release. Follow the healing steps to release what you are experiencing.

What to Do When...

1. When the person needs to feel the love of a distant family member, imagine Jesus putting His hand on the person and another hand on the family member. Thank Jesus for being a Protector from the hurt and a Connector of His love to both of you. Use the Love Hug and Love Pat with slow, gentle pats on the arm as you see and feel this image.

2. After the person releases the negative emotion and is feeling better, ask what they see on their face in the memory? Do they see a flat look or a smile look? A flat look usually indicates sadness or disappointment. Continue using the healing steps to find another early hurtful memory. A smile indicates the release was successful and you can continue to another traumatic event if the condition is not healed.

3. When the person has many layers from multiple hurtful events, they will first release sadness, then disappointment, and then anger before they can forgive. These emotions are usually released one at a time. Use the healing steps to identify the feelings with each event.

4. When the person says they cannot forgive, use the healing steps to find the event and release the emotion from

that event. After releasing the emotion, if they do forgive but still have emotions against the offender, that is evidence that the emotion was not released from the heart. Use the healing steps to find the event where the person was hurt by the offender and release the emotion from that event. If the emotion will not release, expand your search for an earlier hurtful event with similar emotions.

5. When the person tells you that they feel an emotion, pain, or another sensation is being released from their body, you can use a hand motion, such as a very gentle/light brushing off of their shoulders or head. This gentle brushing can be a real or symbolic motion that is wiping away whatever does not belong to the person. While you use the hand motions you can command, "In Jesus' name I release the feeling of "_____." Or "In Jesus' name, I command anything not of God to go and not return." For reasons of respect and to avoid additional trauma, I recommend ONLY touching the head and shoulders while using hand motions.

6. When the person releases the hurt emotion, I recommend you instruct him or her to use the Love Pat repetitions slowly and gently as they see the safe person or Jesus giving them a hug and telling them positive comments to encourage them. This is also a time when the healer can give a positive or uplifting word.

Self-Care Prayer with Love Hug-Love Pat and Visual Release

These steps can be used with yourself or with others:

After you have read this guide book and are comfortable using the healing steps, these Self-Care Healing Steps can be used as a quick reference.

As you sit in a private, comfortable place, think of what your physical or emotional situation makes you feel (i.e., anxious, depressed, hurt, etc.) or describe what it is like living with your condition (i.e., helpless, stuck, etc.).

- Ask God to take you where the emotion and hurt(s) started in your early years.
- After you picture the early hurtful event, measure the amount of emotion you would have felt during the event on a scale from 0 to 10 (10 being the highest amount of emotional hurt).
- Think of a safe person who has been in your life who has provided comfort (anyone from your past or present, i.e., grandparent or Jesus).
- Imagine the safe person comforting you with a hug as they stand between you and the hurtful situa-

tion. To help you experience the hug, cross your arms over your chest, resting your hands on the outside of your arms or bicep (this is called a Love Hug.)

- Next, imagine the safe person comforting you with a gentle pat on your arms. [Your hands can pat your arms as you think of the safe person saying—*you are loved*. This is called a Love Pat, by alternating the patting of your arms.]
(OPTION—As you view the hurtful event, slowly move your eyes to the left and then right to determine on which side you feel and see the event more intensely. Keep looking to the intense side as you use the Love Hug and Love Pat.)

- As you receive the Love Hug and Love Pat, envision yourself handing the hurtful feelings to the safe person as you say what you feel, i.e., *I give you this feeling of*_____.

- Keep using the Love Pat as you allow the thoughts and feelings to flow until you feel or envision the younger image of yourself becoming safer and the emotion decreases to 0 or 1 (on a 0-to-10 scale).

HELPFUL HINTS

- Even if you cannot actually feel the emotion from that event, just see the event and allow the younger you (in the past image) to guess what the feelings would have been when you were in that hurtful situation.

- Whatever negative images, thoughts, or emotions come to mind, speak them aloud as if you are telling the safe person.

- If you cannot think of a safe person, imagine yourself in a "bullet-proof" bubble where you can see the hurtful situation outside the bubble but cannot be touched by it.
- If the feelings get worse, continue doing the Love Pat, saying aloud what you feel.

Prayer details are in Craig's book *Breaking Emotional Barriers to Healing* [paperback, Kindle, ebook, and audio on Amazon]. For more, see Craig's website: insightsfromtheheart.com Craig Miller©2020.

About the Author

CRAIG MILLER has been ministering and counseling in church, medical, and mental health settings since 1980. He is a licensed Christian therapist and co-founder of Masterpeace Counseling in Tecumseh, Michigan. He holds a master's degree in social work from Michigan State University and a master's degree in health services administration from the University of Detroit. He has served as a lay minister and as the director of social work for Herrick Hospital in Tecumseh. Experiencing his own miraculous physical healing deepened Craig's passion to help people receive healing and restoration through teaching, imparting, and ministering the love and healing power of Jesus. Craig ministers to the spirit and soul (mind, will, and emotions) for God to identify the root causes that block healing of physical or emotional conditions. He also teaches and ministers through TV and radio appearances, speaking at national healing conferences and healing services, and is the author of several books.

For more information about Craig, go to:
www.insightsfromtheheart.com

Books available by Craig Miller
www.insightsfromtheheart.com

Breaking Emotional Barriers to Healing: Understanding the Mind/Body Connection to Your Illness. This book teaches how to minister to the spirit and soul to identify root causes that block your emotional and physical healing. Learn effective prayers for bringing permanent solutions to long-term pain and suffering, with real-life testimonies and descriptions of how emotions block healing of over 450 medical conditions. English, Spanish, and Portuguese versions are available.

Finding Victory When Healing Doesn't Happen—This book co-authored with Randy Clark, includes why healing doesn't happen; why you lose your healing; how to pray for specific emotional/physical conditions; changing the atmosphere to believe; praying through issues of unworthiness, unbelief, fear, doubt, curses, spiritual warfare, unforgiveness, real-life healing testimonies and descriptions of emotional connection linked to medical conditions. English and Portuguese versions are available.

Declaring Your Worth—Read powerful miracle stories to learn how to use your authority and power from God. Learn how to pray and declare for your healing, using powerful declarations to read over yourself based on Scriptures to declare that you are worthy, lovable, significant, blameless, accepted, forgiven, set free, victorious, purposeful, confident, attractive, hopeful, blessed, and more. English and Spanish versions are available.

When Your Mate is Emotionally Unavailable—For relationships where the lack of emotions, love, and affection continues despite repeated unsuccessful efforts to change the relationship. Identifies characteristics of living with an emotionally unavailable mate, such as: how you become unemotional, why you love them, negative impact on the family, finding hope, and steps to make radical changes. Questions are included after each chapter for personal or group study.

When Feelings Don't Come Easy—Explains why people struggle to freely express emotions. How emotional suffering, physical and emotional ailments, poor self-worth, and dissatisfaction with life are caused by the lack of expressing feelings. Learn how to identify and express feelings, receive confidence, stop becoming hurt by what others say, and feel better about yourself! Questions are included after each chapter for personal or group study.

CPSIA information can be obtained
at www.ICGtesting.com
Printed in the USA
FSHW021947111121